KNICKS LEGENDS ALPHABET

Words by Robin Feiner

Aa

A is for Carmelo **A**nthony. Melo's 2011 move to New York sent shockwaves throughout the NBA. One of the game's most legendary scorers, Anthony was an All-Star in each of his six full Knicks seasons. His arrival brought hope and star power back to New York – but little playoff success.

Bb

B is for Bill Bradley. Playing his entire 1967–77 career with New York, Bradley did all the little things well and helped the Knicks win the 1970 and 1973 titles. Dollar Bill had a legendary ability to read the game and later became a US Senator.

C is for **C**azzie Russell. Whether as Jazzy Cazzie or Muscle Russell, this forward was drilling long-range jumpers before the three-point line even existed. The 1966 No. 1 overall pick spent his first five seasons in New York, where his legendary bench scoring was key to the Knicks' 1970 title run.

D is for **D**ave DeBusschere. With his physical defense, this legend could take away his opponents' first, second, third, and fourth moves. Big D was the heart and soul of the early 1970s Knicks. An All-Star in each of his five full New York seasons, he helped the team win two titles.

Ee

E is for Patrick Ewing.
One of the best bigs ever
and arguably the greatest
Knick, this legend holds team
records for points, rebounds,
blocks, and steals. Big Pat's
1985–2000 New York tenure
was one of the team's greatest
eras. All that's missing from
this Knickerbocker's career
is a title.

F is for Walt **F**razier. Smooth on and off the court, Frazier was the toast of 1970s New York. His fashion sense earned him the nickname Clyde, while on the court he led the Knicks to two titles. Now a beloved broadcaster, Frazier's colorful outfits are as legendary as his Hall of Fame play.

G is for Harry Gallatin. The Knicks rode The Horse to hundreds of wins and three straight Finals appearances in his nine New York seasons from 1948–57. A bruising rebounder and seven-time All-Star despite his rather small frame, this hard-working legend set a record for consecutive games played with a streak of 610.

H is for Allan **H**ouston. Houston provided crucial outside shooting in the late 1990s. Perhaps the only thing better than his one-handed running jumper to seal the 1999 playoffs series win, is his legendary fist pump celebration. If only his knees had held up.

I is for Iman Shumpert. Shump was a great perimeter defender who helped the Knicks make the playoffs in his first two seasons. But his most legendary contribution might've been creating #Knickstape to describe the mix of players on the popular 2012–13 team that won 54 games.

J is for Mark Jackson. A Brooklyn-born baller, Jackson is one of the greatest point guards for a team with a legendary lack of good ball handlers. He wasn't the biggest on the court. But Jackson embodied the spirit of New York hoops with his tough, physical style of play.

K is for Bernard **K**ing. Despite knee injuries, this hometown hero could flat-out score. King's play during the 1984 playoffs nearly took the Knicks to the Finals, while his legendary turnaround jumper helped him capture the 1984–85 scoring title. King's 60 points on Christmas 1984 are a gift NY hoops fans still haven't forgotten.

L is for Larry Johnson.
Back problems robbed this
once-dynamic power forward
of a greater career. But he'll
always be a Knicks legend,
famous for his four-point
play in the dying moments
of Game 3 of the 1999 Eastern
Conference Finals. People say
Madison Square Garden has
never been louder.

M is for Earl 'The Pearl' **M**onroe. Once a rival, Monroe became a Knicks legend after joining the team in 1971. His dazzling style of play changed what guards were capable of, and his pairing with the silky smooth Walt Frazier helped New York win the 1973 title.

N is for Willie **N**aulls. Naulls shot his way to four All-Star teams playing mostly for bad 1950s and 1960s Knicks teams. But perhaps his most legendary feat was becoming team captain in 1960, making him the first black captain of a major US sports team according to the Knicks.

Oo

O is for Charles Oakley. One of the game's last true enforcers, Oak is known for his legendary toughness. Helping New York make the playoffs each year of his 1988–98 Knicks career, Oakley and Patrick Ewing made every trip to the rim a nightmare for opponents.

P is for **P**at Riley.
During his 1991–95 Knicks tenure, Pat Riley brought legendary toughness and pedigree to a franchise that couldn't get past the second round. He guided four 50-plus-win seasons and a long-awaited NBA Finals return. Riley abruptly left on bad terms. But the memories remain.

Qq

Q is for Immanuel **Q**uickley. This member of the 2020–21 All-Rookie Team is a sneaky good rebounder and defender who showed flashes of brilliance early in his career. But it's legendarily tough for younger players to find the court when coach Tom Thibodeau insists on playing veterans heavy minutes.

HOLZMAN
613
KNICKS

Rr

R is for Red Holzman. The first – and for decades only – man to bring ultimate basketball glory to New York. This legend's 613 Knicks head coaching wins are a franchise record. His philosophy built on pressure defense and team play propelled 1970 and 1973 title teams full of icons to the top.

S is for John Starks.
A spark off the bench for the 1990s Knicks, Starks' toughness made him a New York legend even when others outside the city doubted him. This shooting guard's streakiness was a gift and a curse. But his dunk over Michael Jordan in the 1993 playoffs remains an iconic piece of hoops history.

T is for Kurt **T**homas.
This bruising power forward put his hand up to do the dirty work after legendary enforcer Charles Oakley left the team. Thomas was willing to bop any opponent coming down the lane. He dished out plenty of punishment during New York's highs and lows from 1998–2005.

U is for Richie Guerin.
A six-time All-Star from
1957–63, this native
New Yorker was a fiery
competitor. Despite a lot
of losing, the Hall of Famer
became a local legend by
leaving it all on the floor
and leading the Knicks in
scoring and assists for four
straight seasons.

V is for Jeff **V**an Gundy. The Knicks went 225–153 in his five full New York head coaching seasons from 1996–2001. A legendary Diet Coke drinker, Van Gundy preached defense – infamously trying to play some himself on Alonzo Mourning during a 1998 playoff series brawl.

W is for **W**illis Reed. Hobbling out for Game 7 of the 1970 Finals and inspiring the Knicks to their first title is legendary enough. But The Captain, a seven-time All-Star and two-time NBA Finals MVP, played his entire 10-year career in New York before knee injuries cruelly ended it at the young age of 32.

Xx

X is for Xavier McDaniel.
X-Man started the entire
1991–92 season, his only
one for New York. He was
then tasked with hounding
the Bulls' Scottie Pippen in a
grueling seven-game playoff
series, in which he also went
face-to-face with Michael
Jordan. The Knicks lost, but
McDaniel made his mark.

Y is for "**Y**es, and it counts!"
One of basketball's most
legendary catchphrases,
New York hoops fans heard
this iconic call from Marv
Albert countless times during
his run as the voice of the
Knicks from 1967–2004.
An all-time great, Albert laid
the foundation for many of
today's best broadcasters.

Z is for Max Zaslofsky. A potent scorer in his day, Zaslofsky always seemed to wriggle free for his signature two-handed set shot. Slats played three seasons in New York from 1950–53, helping lead the team to the 1953 Finals and earning an All-Star nod along the way.

The ever-expanding legendary library

EXPLORE THESE LEGENDARY ALPHABETS & MORE AT WWW.ALPHABETLEGENDS.COM

KNICKS LEGENDS ALPHABET
www.alphabetlegends.com

Published by Alphabet Legends Pty Ltd in 2023
Created by Beck Feiner
Copyright © Alphabet Legends Pty Ltd 2023

Printed and bound in China.

9780645851441